The Idea of Leaves within the Dying Tree

poems by

Brendan Todt

Finishing Line Press
Georgetown, Kentucky

The Idea of Leaves within the Dying Tree

Copyright © 2016 by Brendan Todt
ISBN 978-1-944251-41-3 First Edition
All rights reserved under International and Pan-American Copyright Conventions.
No part of this book may be reproduced in any manner whatsoever without written permission from the publisher, except in the case of brief quotations embodied in critical articles and reviews.

ACKNOWLEDGMENTS

The author would like to thank the editors of the following journals in which some of these pieces first appeared, sometimes in slightly different forms:

Chronogram: "Pheasant on a Postcard from Iowa City"
Glassworks: "The Best Week" and "Chinese Parsley"
South Dakota Review: "In Times like These"

Editor: Christen Kincaid

Cover Art: DJ Todt

Author Photo: DJ Todt

Cover Design: Elizabeth Maines

Printed in the USA on acid-free paper.
Order online: www.finishinglinepress.com
also available on amazon.com

Author inquiries and mail orders:
Finishing Line Press
P. O. Box 1626
Georgetown, Kentucky 40324
U. S. A.

Table of Contents

Late Middle Age as a Cool Place in the Shade 1

In Times like These 2

All the Little Flowers 3

Uncle Bwendan 4

We Stop on the Hiking Trail to Observe a Sleeping Doe 5

For a Moment I Thought It Might Really Have Happened 6

Condition of the Field after the Sun Has Been Removed 7

The Cottage at Pheasant Lake 8

To the College Students Stuffed Uneasily into Their Easy Chair ... 9

Love Poem at High Tide 11

Big Island Falls 13

Cold, Dry Air 15

When We Walk to the River 16

The Human Condition 17

The Best Week 18

The Stars as Seen from Here 19

Against Epiphany 21

The Second Year 23

Chinese Parsley 25

A Place for His Toothbrush 26

As the Weather Turns Cold 27

Pheasant on a Postcard from Iowa City 28

*the feeling of something
important gone missing. That roots' good
intentions aren't always enough. That always
is only ever intention.*

Monica Berlin
&
Beth Marzoni

LATE MIDDLE AGE AS A COOL PLACE THE SHADE

This will not last. The earth will twist
about its axis and the shade will leave me
here, exposed. Or worse, the clouds will gather,
as they often do, and replace the tree's
shade with their own. This is what
we are all headed for. And this is the only
humane way to speak of love and nature.
The one consumes the other.
Not out of spite—necessarily—or even hunger.
These are the wrong words because they are the closest words.
I chose my tree because it was in the park
and overlooked a fountain.
There were several others: trees and fountains.
Leaves and colorful aluminum pipes
bent into shapes only a child
as flexible as his imagination
could fit into. The only space left for me
to fill is this shade, and standing back up
has become as difficult as keeping pace
with the earth as it moves, simultaneously
taking me with it and leaving me behind.

IN TIMES LIKE THESE

It's hard to believe that the world goes on spinning
cluelessly around us. That our best friends
did not pick up the hints and cancel
the dinner at Madigan's I made reservations for
two weeks ago. Of course they didn't.
This isn't the same world now is it?
The paintings on the wall don't occupy
the same delicate coordinates they used to.
Here we are at Madigan's on a Thursday night
looking into the mirror on the other side of the room.
Neither of us is as good looking as we used to be.
Or as honest. I should have stopped you before you left
the house in your peanut-colored dress. Before you
ordered your second and then third glasses of Malbec.
I should not have laughed at that story you told about Bill
and neither of us should pretend we'll take the check
when Jeff and Abby make like they will pay.

ALL THE LITTLE FLOWERS

At the swimming hole the long
silver blue mirror of the water.
Convex and in turns concave.
Children jumping into their many
distorted shapes reflected in it.
Cannon balls and swan dives.
The belly flop.
They emerge from the water
holding onto the simplest of truths:
water is always wet
and the pond like their mothers
will always make room for them.

Water sloshes up over the sandals
of the babysitters waiting
to drive the children back home.
Some girls have dreams of their own.
The married men they work for.
The slim wrists of the women.
The briefcases with locks and keys.

In their own backyards before dinner
they will sit in their lawn chairs
and take off their sundresses.
Bathing suit tops and bottoms
bright with stripes
or the round edges of flowers
as only children can draw them.
The babysitters adjust their chairs,
always wanting the sun in their face.
The sun moves like the hands of clocks,
not counting
up or down to anything.

UNCLE BWENDAN

I pulled my chair up to the kids' table.
They told me I'd have to bring them
their plates of food: honey ham, yams,
corn bread, carrots, *no green beans*.
Then they'd need their vodka and tonics.
And finally their desserts.
Kids can eat and drink a lot.
Then it was time for presents
and I had to pull each one of them
out from under the tree.
I was told to go out for batteries
and cigarettes, and that I would have to cross
into Indiana because they refused to pay
the enormous cigarette tax in Illinois.
One of them gave me a five
for the toll and extra effort.
It all seemed reasonable enough.
Winter is like dying which is like
every moment of being a child;
it keeps going
away and going away and only when
your brothers and sisters
have kids of their own do you think
maybe you can get it back.
I left what remained of the five
with the toll clerk. It was Christmas.
No one should have to work
like a child works.

WE STOP ON THE HIKING TRAIL TO OBSERVE A SLEEPING DOE

What if what we are looking for,
when we arrive at it, is not alive?
No matter how much we talked

about the felled log looking like
a quiet or injured deer, it was not.

No matter how we ridiculed ourselves
or exaggerated the story to others,

no matter how cautiously we approached
the old log, still believing:

You, who have asked me to write
poems about many things,
and I, who could not;

We, who love devoutly
this physical empirical world
and go to sleep each night

grateful that the world has not yet

asked us to define
what it is or what
we are incapable of being.

FOR A MOMENT I THOUGHT IT MIGHT REALLY HAVE HAPPENED

Neutrinos, we're learning,
can't really be stopped
by anything
except sometimes by luck.
We build walls of lead
tens of feet thick
and that's how we think
we will learn the mind of god.
For a moment it appeared
we were onto something
and they could travel, like souls,
faster than the speed of light.
Neutrinos shot in grand
experiments
from Geneva to Gran Sasso.
Batavia to somewhere
in cold Minnesota.
Patrons of the honest
Midwestern work ethic.
Modest, nearly
invisible.
Billions of them
passing through me
every second.
The odd one left behind
in some fat around
the kidney is all the god
I suspect
I shall ever need.

CONDITION OF THE FIELD AFTER THE SUN HAS BEEN REMOVED

The rat comes. And the hawk pursuing the rat.
The neighbors sit on their porch
imagining themselves as hawks
swooping into the field,
coming up with a rat for dinner.

Now the travelers come,
passing by on State Highway 41,
wishing they could live
someplace like this,
imagining what it would be like

to be themselves,
stopped for a moment
and sitting on a porch
with two lemonades
like rats in their hands.

THE COTTAGE AT PHEASANT LAKE

It's been weeks since we've talked seriously
about the cottage at Pheasant Lake.
Mentioned the willows or small-stone walkway.
Weeks since we've done other things:
walked outside, gone together to the theater, arrived jovially
someplace we never would have expected, like the Mennonite
restaurant in Lavonia.

It's a shame,
watching the big red belly of the sun set every day.
I know it's in everyone's nature to leave. The sun.
My buddy Greg I shoot baskets with.
My mother leaves for work every day
convinced she's not coming back.

So is it the sun, or gravity,
or a diamond glinting like what I mistook for the fish
of Pheasant Lake keeping us together?
It's this implacable need I have for her
to fill my outer orbits with her electrons.
So we can dance like children
dream of dancing, quickly, manic, and at speeds
and with such beauty
no one can say for certain
where we have been or where
we might be going.

TO THE COLLEGE STUDENTS STUFFED UNEASILY INTO THEIR EASY CHAIR

I've seen it before: this love.
The one-on-top-of-the-other,
cram-it-all-in, no-chair-
is-large-enough-to-contain-us mush.
Eventually the legs hurt.
All the sitting.
Pain, in this way,
is not unrelated to love.
It is like looking at love from space.
Sometimes the one is all you can see of the other:
like the pyramids. And great storms.
We are lucky
that most great storms pass.
We have so few words left
for love that we have taken
to calling the great storm on Jupiter
an eye.
Some loves are great
storms that do not pass.
Others are ugly arm chairs
that mean well and are only comfortable
when you are not sitting on them
but sitting on someone
who is sitting on them.
I was mistaken.
It is not the planet that has an eye.
The eye is in the weather above the planet.
Like one lover on top of the other
on top of the chair.
If I tell you I have never been touched
by any one or thing, will you think
I am as empty as I am?

The theorists now theorize
that our most fundamental particles will never
touch a single other in their lifetimes.
My god, wasn't it cliché enough
when we were told we were made up of love?
Even more now that we are nothing but
empty space? Like the gap between
two teeth the lover loves but doesn't
know why. Or the uncomfortable crevasse
that opens up between the seat
and the back of the chair when it reclines,
where his keys and phone and sense
of logic, if he had one, disappear.
These are not black holes.
The only mysteries we have left
are what to call things.
Your mother calls it a loveseat.
Your father puppy love.
The dentist, diastema.
And I say you are mine,
though the storm roaring down
the mountain suggests otherwise.

LOVE POEM AT HIGH TIDE

Cold air sinks, the heart does too,
and on the moon a day can last a year.
The waves on the beach leave
and wander back and we wonder why
water makes us think of sex.

Water and the moon. Cold air,
colder hearts. Who needs whom
more, the seer or the seen?
Before the paramecia emerged
were the stars like other universes
just waiting to be perceived?

And were you really happy
in his well-evolved arms
or were you merely standing in
what you thought was an ocean
but wasn't yet, and wouldn't be,
until the sea crept in and in the moonlight
you found me?

Let's take this moment and stick
our hands into the sand for clams.
Because so much of what we are is buried
underneath.
I know it wasn't really me you found.
I wasn't there. Nor you.
The earth was lively and fragrant and more so
because there were so many of us
reflected in the waters breaking forth.

Before you I'd never seen an ocean;
never been one. There are things that float
and those that sink and the rest
rest only on the surface:
the moon and stars and the vast
black spaces I told you I would fill
even if it took, like the ocean,
all my breath.

BIG ISLAND FALLS

In tiers the walls and water drop.
They stay upright best
and only in our memories.
I was there, remember this.
The food tasted like—I wore—we kissed.
The sun stayed up then down
exactly as long as we needed.
We slept—or didn't. Told stories.
Made up our past and recalled our futures.
In between there were bed sheets and coasters
and the telephone interrupting.
I asked who someone was
though I thought I knew.
I did and didn't. It was a friend,
a woman, but younger and sadder.
If that was her, then what's become
of us since dawn and scrambled eggs?
How has the rain changed us?
How does the rain change itself
from cloud to leaf to leaf to ground?
What river did we stand in last night?
What bathtub? Who emerged,
what towel dried, and once the water's swallowed
what happens to us then?
We've heard and read enough
we're mostly water. How much,
how often, why? You held my hand
and when you cried did you
become more or less yourself?
Spring will come and floods
will kill and in summer, somewhere,
a man will breathe in dust.

I can live with and without so many things.
Water may be one of them.
And you might be, too. But who cares
to think like that when the river leaps
below us with such abandon
it does not matter who
or what will catch it?

COLD, DRY AIR

I've had my share of cracked
and bloody knuckles running
miles along the lake in February.

Waves break—what a way to put it—
against the concrete moors along the trail.
Never has a wave not broken.

It must be in the wave's nature to break.
The hands' to bleed.
The wife's to bend at the waist

and dab the blood
out of love.

WHEN WE WALK TO THE RIVER

The barge drifts by. My mind
is a tiny place but not so
tiny as the captain's quarters.

The river passes us, engineered
by a couple of drops trickling down the mountains.

There is something to be said
about the placement of stones
lining the walking path
that leads us to the river,
but that thing has yet to be said.

Soon the old tug is gone. Upstream
we hear another.
A dog walks up to us and we pet her
and then she leaves.
That is the nature of the river.

THE HUMAN CONDITION

Think of the cadaver dogs, the weeks
of training, praise, and chicken liver treats.
The exotic smell of decomposing human
remains that to a dog must smell like

pornography. Think of having a purpose,
finally, after a life
lived without one; it's astonishing
how many of these dogs are rescues.

Think of the pride of leading
the hundred-yard-wide search party
through the marsh beyond I-29
and the glitch in your canine olfactory

when you smell her eight-year-old
skin in the soft loam near some lichen,
and stand with your nose to the ground
but like a good dog, do not dig.

THE BEST WEEK

A girl will struggle in the water on the evening news.
Her father will jump in to help and fail.
The helicopter pilot ten months from her pension
will swing the red swimmer through the canopy
and into the water where he will have to choose
who to swim to first.
I will watch it all in passing as you stir fry our vegetables
and call you in to see how the father goes under
and comes up and goes under again
and to ask you how
the network can show something like that on TV.
I'll add more peppers to the wok and stand behind you
as the grease teases our arms with something we can't quite call pain.
For eight days we will fight and storm out
and make up as we never have before,
as if it were the water we were battling
on behalf of the father, and the mother who by now
has emptied and rinsed and recycled his toiletries
and is absolutely convinced
she will never speak to her daughter
or go to the river or have curry, which was his favorite, again.
You will come home to fresh squash and fileted salmon
and for those eight days you'll eat better and you won't know why.
The sky above the house will change as it always does,
and I will attribute it to turmeric and paprika
and the restaurant owner's lemon-scented dish soap
whirlpooling together with a missing left shoe
past the grates of the bakeries downtown.

THE STARS AS SEEN FROM HERE

Fires light in barrels and pillow
up from stacks of burning pallets.
Two loaves of bread and half
a pack of processed cheese.
I've seen the flames and glow.
It's not ugly, you know,
in a city with no visible stars.
If someone's lucky enough not to have
bartered away their last tomato,
then there's that to look forward to, too.
One slice per child per family.
The matches strike.
Some rent-a-cop arrives and chases them away.
Families in constellations of fires
moving night
after night from park to park
to parking lot. The path of despair
is the path of the stars first
tracked by the ancients on stone tablets.
Like a stone, little changes
have big consequences: Over time.
In the Badlands, I saw firsthand
the thirty-foot hoodoo give way.
The sound broke more than anything.
It's unfair
to say the heart breaks. It doesn't.
The muscle tears. Like pieces of newspaper
used for kindling when not
serving as the makeshift stuffing of a coat.
After a nice dinner with my wife, we stopped
and gave a woman on a bench our leftovers.
We thought that was how things got moving.

No one's life was changed
but maybe mine.
A woman ate that night. She wouldn't the next.
The stars themselves weren't moving.
The Mesopotamians and Greeks only
thought they were and best of all
had yet to realize theirs
were the feet wandering about the sky.
They thought their prayers to the mountain
gods brought bountiful harvests.
And maybe they did. Now double-
blind studies suggest prayer helps
patients in long-term recoveries.
But haven't we learned
it's not who we're talking to that matters most?
If I'm being honest I wasn't
feeding the woman but myself,
as I had at the restaurant
and would again with a snack before bed.
There must have been people in the early days—
even now—who thought the stars really disappeared
when they closed their eyes or shook their hands in front of them.
It's nice to think we have such power.
The next morning a couple of families
pulled their campers off the road
and with some chains and winches tried
to raise the latest monument to movability.
The park rangers, who knew better, just watched.
And I watched them watch, and came home,
and split the drive with my wife
so one or the other of us could rest
our eyes a while longer.

AGAINST EPIPHANY

Like getting her away from the kids and in the back of the theater
    parking lot
parking with the teenage kids, rocking our sedan a little, going places
    on our bodies,
not like running errands or going for a walk,
but going like she tells me she does when she should be working,
into the timber behind the hospital, forgetting
the terminal patients placed there overlooking it.

Like the dog rooting under the couch for what I was sure was a
    tennis ball or an old treat she had dropped
and when I get up and get the kids up and the three of us lift in
    unison and find nothing,
only partially like that, because we rarely know what we are missing.
Not like being in the forest and finding a bird, or being in the forest
    and finding a polished, dismantled, Russian-made
    Kalishnakov.
Like being in the forest and finding another human being so much
    like yourself
it is so obvious you are the imposter
you must follow yourself to the creek bed and only then question
    why
you have never been there before.

Not like being in these bodies, or like building them, deconstructing
    them,
not like burying or burning or drawing them naked with charcoal on
    the south wall of a Korean grocery.
Not like smelling the button of a melon and getting the timing
    wrong—yes, like getting the timing wrong!—

like realizing when you bring the melon home it was the wrong
    melon, that somewhere on the pyramid of melons is your
    melon,
your perfectly ripe and chosen melon, the melon you are cutting in
    your head and delivering on teak toothpicks to your wife
who has simultaneously destroyed and caricatured your body in ash,
    in sidewalk chalk on the driveway,
where our daughters are playing together in the sun
already dying of happiness and envisioning
a forest in which they can hide from us sprawled out endlessly
    beneath them.

THE SECOND YEAR

I crouched on my knees
scrubbing and thinking about how I proposed.
From there I could see the baseboard
didn't meet flush against the north wall of the guest room.
The next day a bulb burned out.
A week later one of the toilets wouldn't flush.
We held hands on the drive to the hardware store
so worried we were that something was coming between us.

At dinner we sat on the same side of the booth
like all the weirdoes we'd always poked fun of.
I asked if it was okay to tip this much;
you said yes; we did not want to anger each other.

We fed ourselves better.
More vegetables, less red meat.
Our lives improved.
Other lights burned out. We returned
to the hardware store. Summer arrived.
After an open, honest conversation,
we opened the windows. Our allergies flared.

In a park along the river you opened your blouse.
I sneezed at the crocus, then smiled.
Autumn and an album full of photographs of leaves.
Rustic dresses. The word *crimson*.
The smoky taste of burnt leaves filling
the neighborhood. We closed the windows.
I burned the Thanksgiving turkey.
We opened them again.

Winter and Christmas. The days lengthening.
We spend less time in the drab bedroom.
We open the blinds to let some light in.
I cook more. You fold clothes on the couch.
We watch a couple of Bowl games,
March Madness. I ask if you heard
Arlington declared for the draft.
You had. I have another question
which I've forgotten. It will come back to me,
you say, it always does.

CHINESE PARSLEY

I've heard it's not necessary
to know a language
in order to translate from it

which makes me believe
maybe we're not so bad
off after all

and what we're doing
by loving

is taking each other
one word at a time
and looking it up

and allowing ourselves
to deviate from the actual,
literal thing—baby,
my actual,

literal heart has never
actually, literally ached
for you—

with something that has more
to do with coriander

being no more than the seeds
of the cilantro plant, another
name for the herb

we once tried to grow
on the windowsill,
cooking and smelling happy,

if that makes any sense.

A PLACE FOR HIS TOOTHBRUSH

There's something about the way she touches
her nose to signal to him it is time
to exeunt party left, pick up
that liter of gin they had talked about,
take their clothes off, shower, make love,
and then shower again.

Something about the way she uses
the word torque out of context
that makes him think of elbow grease
and the couple of stains left
on the couch the night
they both fell off of it.

Something about the way they fuck
with all the lights on and then laugh
at how poorly the video turned out.
About the way she walks around with a towel on
afterward, and how she asks him to leave
when she uses the bathroom.

Something about turning the pancakes over
and seeing that he has burnt them.
About placing them on a separate plate
so that he can eat them before she comes into the room.

Something that is part but not the whole story of love,
the charred taste in his mouth he can't get out
after any number of G&Ts, mouthwash,
maple syrup or sleep.

AS THE WEATHER TURNS COLD

I built a fire in the new house.
She said she wouldn't know
until morning whether she liked it or not.
It all depended on how the kitchen smelled
and what kind of mess I'd made.
The next morning she said it was fine,
but the moment I got back from taking
the dog around the block I could smell
everything wrong that I had missed.
This is the fire people mean when they talk about love.
Not white hot flames and not candles
floating in bathtubs; the faint odor
of burned wet wood that lingers
well into morning. We'd slept in it
just long enough we didn't notice
anymore what was and wasn't there.
The dog was there, and the snow outside,
and she and I were there,
and the cabinets and the smells,
and the coffee and the smells,
and the plate of ice that fell from the roof
and shattered in the driveway.
The words were there, and the mouths
that made and ate them,
and the bodies that touched like table legs
supporting the hardwood floors.
The day may come we'll have to burn
the furniture just to keep warm.
If it does, we can take comfort in
the possibility there won't be many
left to smell.

PHEASANT ON A POSTCARD FROM IOWA CITY

I talked to a man today, who has been married and divorced, about a woman he is seeing—she is twenty-six—and how he would like and needs to keep her. How he plans to take her to Italy as often as possible and announce to her in a flourish, *I give you Florence, I give you Venice, I give you Rome.* We both know I cannot give you Rome. All I can offer you is Iowa—and this pheasant we will pretend is the wild turkey we saw running along a county highway somewhere in the state of Virginia.

Brendan Todt's poems have appeared in *Ninth Letter, South Dakota Review, Pank, Glassworks Magazine,* and elsewhere. His short fiction can be found as part of the *Tin House Flash Friday Series* and in *NANO Fiction, Potomac Review,* and *Pamplemousse*. A collection of short stories he co-wrote with BJ Hollars was a finalist in the Black Lawrence Press, *Burnside Review,* and *New Delta Review* chapbook competitions. His poem "At the Particle Accelerator at Krasnoyarsk" was included in *Best American Nonrequired Reading* 2013. He teaches Composition and Literature at Western Iowa Tech Community College and referees youth, high school, and college soccer. He lives in Sioux City, Iowa with his wife and son. Read more or contact him at brendantodt.com.

www.ingramcontent.com/pod-product-compliance
Lightning Source LLC
Chambersburg PA
CBHW051705040426
42446CB00009B/1320